Top Reasons Your Business Still Has No Customers

by

Marcus Guiliano

Top Reasons Your Business Still Has No Customers

Copyright © 2018 by Marcus Guiliano

All rights reserved. Printed in the United States of America. No part of this book may be used or reproduced in any manner whatsoever without written permission except in the case of brief quotations embodied in critical articles or reviews.

For information contact:

Marcus@MarcusGuiliano.com

www.50Mistakes.com

Contributing Editor

Carl Solomon

www.SolomonVoiceServices.com

Cover design by Perry Elisabeth Design

www.perryelisabethdesign.com

First Edition: February 2018

10 9 8 7 6 5 4 3 2 1

TABLE OF CONTENTS

FOREWORD 1

PREFACE 4

Reason #1:	Alert…The Internet has no idea you're alive. 6	
Reason #2:	You just need a website these days. 10	
Reason #3:	Get help to target the Internet better. 16	
Reason #4:	Data dictate success. 18	
Reason #5:	You're not the nosey neighbor. 20	
Reason #6:	What light's your fire? Where's your passion? 22	
Reason #7:	What's your story? 27	
Reason #8:	Market your business like you'd spread grass seed: Network 33	
Reason #9:	How mobile is your presence? 38	
Reason #10:	Who's your audience? 41	
Reason #11:	Don't put all your money in one place.. 44	
Reason #12:	What makes you unique? 47	
Final Thoughts	 51	

FOREWORD

HAVE YOU EVER COME across an idea that literally changed the trajectory of your business? If so, you already know the power just one great idea can have on a business – and you're reading a book packed with them.

I'm Tim Paulson, and I've been in the business world for over 35 years. Years ago I served as Vice-President of Hair Club for Men, helping the company go from $8 million a year to over $100 million a year during the years I was there. In recent decades I've traveled around the world writing, speaking and teaching.

I met Marcus Guiliano a decade ago. Since then we've been in attendance at the same business seminar at least 30 times, and he has spoken at many of them. He is a business expert who is much sought out by his peers.

When Marcus speaks, people listen.

People gather around him to discover new insights and experiences he has to share. He's valued because he speaks from his personal experience. You see, Marcus is in the trenches of business every day. Not only does he run a successful restaurant (one of the coolest in New York), he's also a prolific author. He produces training videos, audios, and books – and does live lectures as well. Marcus is a man who is always on the go, diving deep into personal self-improvement which he generously shares with others.

I read an advanced copy of **Top Reasons Your Business Still Has no Customers**, and it's terrific. I've read hundreds of business books throughout my career, and this book is filled with practical advice that business people need to not only know, but will benefit tremendously from implementing. There's no fluff in the book – it's all quick and practical advice.

I love how Marcus doesn't share theory, but only that which he himself has implemented for success in his business.

He's "been there, and done that."

He writes, *"I truly live and eat what I've presented to you."* I'm a witness of the accuracy of that statement. He's direct – he doesn't pull punches, and he's a terrific teacher. His practical advice – ranging from the importance of your business being different than your competition, to valuable resources and technical insights – will be a good reminder to some, and breakthrough thinking for others.

I believe Marcus wrote this book because he has a passion for business, he loves sharing, and he loves to help his fellow entrepreneurs.

Whether you're one who's owned a business for decades, or a brand-new entrepreneur, this book can be invaluable to you.

Tim Paulson

Preface

DURING THE LAST FEW years, I've been heavily into producing audio and video content for YouTube, radio, and my various websites. These generally short, content rich pieces cover a rather wide range: expressing the diversity of my interests and passions. My efforts are targeted for a variety of individuals from health and fitness enthusiasts to those interested in food advocacy issues, as well as, to those who are business oriented. I rely on many outside resources to find inspiration for these productions.

With the recent release of my book *50 Mistakes Business Owners Make*, I wanted to provide readers with a shorter guide containing strategies for how to increase their business' profile in the public's view. Before getting into the specifics of what is to come, first let me make mention of some resources I believe every business owner (current or potential), budding blogger, writer, or researcher should know about.

Among the first of these resources is Google Alerts. Registering with Google Alerts allows you to be able to select your interests, thereby tailoring the information you elect to receive. This provides you with the inherent power of the Internet to garner more for your business, than you could necessarily obtain otherwise.

The inspiration for this writing was an article entitled *Top 10 Reasons Customers Have No Idea Your Business Exists*, written by Hannah Whittenly. You can find the original article here:

http://customerthink.com/top-10-reasons-customers-have-no-idea-your-business-exists/.

As mentioned, I obtain inspiration, "conversation" starters, and research points from the foregoing listed resources. For this expanded writing I was sent Hannah's article via Google Alerts.

I encourage you to not only find your passion, but to enhance and broaden your knowledge of the subject(s) you're interested in, through wise research and leveraging your time through the use of these resources.

Reason #1: Alert...The Internet has no idea you're alive.

LET'S START WITH THE first issue at hand. About six or seven years ago we made the transition to a VoIP phone setup for our business, Aroma Thyme Bistro, removing the traditional landline phone there and in our home. Traditional landline phones are slowly but surely disappearing. In fact, I know of people living in more rural environments than my own, who recently reported to me issues with obtaining traditional copper line phones. You'd think in more rural areas of the country these types of phones would be supported still: to the contrary. More and more the traditional phone is disappearing.

This demonstrates there's an increasing reliance on things Internet based and/or wireless/cell oriented. These technologies are becoming the standard across the entire country even for home security. A perfect example of this is represented with the success of a company like SimpliSafe.

I've also noticed my local White/Yellow pages phone book has gotten increasingly smaller over recent years. This makes some sense, especially in light of the portability and impermanency of people relying more heavily on pay-as-you-go cell phone plans from the likes of Walmart or changing cell phone numbers/carriers as budget and need may allow, thereby foregoing traditional landlines. I've also noticed fewer and fewer people letting their "fingers do the walking" in the traditional format, versus an increase in the use and relative ease of reaching for one's smart phone or tablet to find out the information sought regarding local businesses of all types. One of the best ways to become an Internet friendly, noticeable business is through Google Alerts.

There are two significantly beneficial reasons to utilize Google Alerts. The primary one is so your business can be noticed. You can, and in my opinion, must register your business with Google Alerts. By doing this you put your "storefront" out there for the world to see.

Whether you're a true brick and mortar, without a website (another topic by itself and something I strongly recommend you have for your business) or you have a website that is not active: you need to ensure the information listed on Google Alerts is active, accurate and up-to-date.

Perhaps you're not aware that Google uses your address, area code, type of business (the essential elements making up the characteristics of your business' profile) as search criteria. You won't be found if you're not out there…so get out there! In order to get any "hits", read that as potentially more phone calls regarding you and your services, you need to be out there.

I hate to harp on this, but I'm going to. Without your active involvement and watchful eyes on your presence in cyberspace, you're going to suffer both potential and actual loss to your bottom line. Unless you have some super-duper, amazingly terrific thing going on with your business that keeps you more busy than you can handle simply by word-of-mouth, then you're definitely limiting your profitability overall.

As a business owner, it is also imperative you stay relevant and up-to-date on trends, advances, and latest technologies in your sector of the business world. Google Alerts can serve this purpose for you as well. By registering with the service you'll be able to select, not only areas of personal interest, but perhaps more crucially, areas related (directly and indirectly) to your business.

Google alerts serves as your personal valet, bringing beneficial information directly to you. This is time saving and efficient. It is smart. It is also potentially profitable. As I made note of in *50 Mistakes Business Owners Make*, understanding what is going on in your industry by reading trade journals and going to trade shows is important; Google Alerts is actually an easy and free way of getting more information without having to go out and find it.

Reason #2: You just need a website these days.

I UNDERSTAND YOU might feel overwhelmed with the thought of having a website, but let me put this into greater perspective for you. Just about everyone has a cell phone, and of those who do, most of those are smart phones. In an article published by CNET on June 5, 2013, Dara Kerr noted, "Currently 91 percent of people in the U.S. own a cell phone and 35 percent have some feature phone…While young adults are the highest adopters with around 80 percent owning a smartphone." You can find the full article here:

> https://www.cnet.com/news/smartphone-ownership-reaches-critical-mass-in-the-u-s/.

Given the data are nearly four years old, the obvious purchasing trend has been higher for replacing older cell phone technologies with smartphones: the 80 percent reference has only risen. Add to that the dramatic increase in the purchase and use of tablet based devices and you have a population of folks who are ever more connected than before. Oh, need I also mention the dramatic rise in Wi-Fi connected businesses?

I'm hoping you see a pretty picture beginning to develop and you're anticipating where I'm going with this. Joe and Jane Public go to their favorite restaurant, local watering hole, or may be sitting in their respective doctor's office waiting room. They need to find "x" service business. No phone books around. No reason to dial 411. They simply take out their smart device connect to the local public Wi-Fi network and presto: the top 10 related businesses in their local area pop up, replete with address, phone, website information, and local ratings from those who have used the respective services.

Your business either doesn't show up because you failed to register with Google Alerts or it does and there is no website to go check out. Let's say it's the latter. Joe and Jane see three other businesses with ratings and websites. They check out these three and select one or two to call. Truly, this is not a far-fetched scenario. In fact this scenario plays out regularly. Sadly, your business is not even given a chance. You've missed the opportunity to gain new business.

It is no longer acceptable, especially if you're paying for a brick and mortar facility, not having a website. You need not be tech savvy as there are those who can help you. In fact, even if you're totally a rank novice or someone with even less experience than that, you can build and launch your own website and make it look quite professional.

Admittedly, I have some experience in this area, but once upon a time I didn't. Foreseeing where the trend in the business world was going, I invested a portion of my time learning how to use almost all of this technology. I wanted to be self-sufficient, position my business so it had a significant internet presence, and ensure my profitability. Currently, I use some professional services to assist me in launching and/or managing the websites I've created. I've recently made efforts to reconstruct the look of all of my websites. I've found hosting services like FatCow.com, Weebly.com, and Wix.com to be relatively easy to use. Each has excellent customer service and technical support. If after viewing the aforementioned resources you don't find the feel/look to your liking, simply conduct an Internet search for the *Top 10* services in each area and give them a call. There are many other hosting and website creation services available offering excellent value.

Let me offer a crucial word regarding the name of your domain/website. First off, people are more likely to remember your website name than your phone number: yet another reason a website is a critical tool for your business. Be prepared at this juncture in our society's technological march for your business name to perhaps be already in use. You may need to get creative with regard to the naming of your website in order to zero in on something that is easily remembered, identifiable for your business, and not already taken. It is a bit late in the game to find "obvious" domain names in most standard industry/professional sectors. Don't lose heart. I'm sure you've got good people around you who'd be more than willing to lend a helping hand. Additionally, you could potentially gain the assistance of your previous clientele: especially those who are repeat users of your services. You can use this level of rapport as potential leverage later in your promotional activity.

For those of you who are just starting out on the road to business ownership and you have yet to think in these terms, or have the attitude that a website is something you can put off until later, take note of the following. You're making a huge and horribly costly mistake! You need your website now and should be planning to launch it long before you open your doors.

Let's consider the rationale for building and launching your website prior to opening your doors. The clothing industry is a great example of marketing long before the actual need arises. Generally, you'll find that summer clothing is marketed and put in stores long before spring is over. By doing this, designers and retail outlets create anticipation, excitement and generally sales in advance of the coming season. Clothing is not the only industry to conduct business in this manner. Just about every sector of the retail market begins advertising before the product is on the street. Your new business launch should be no different.

You need to take advantage of the time prior to your grand opening to create anticipation, excitement, and desire to utilize your services. By promoting your new business through your website prior to opening, you may persuade someone or frankly several to many someones to wait for your services over a business already open. The manner in which you "pre-sell" who you are is so important that it can't be overstated.

Reason #3: Get help to target the Internet better.

THE INTERNET CAN BE your greatest resource or it can become the bane of your existence. If you're one of those individuals who are technically savvy, able to create your own website, embed the proper key wording for each of the pages, and maximize your internet exposure: then you can pass over this section.

The essential first step in using the Internet to best advantage your business is through SEO or Search Engine Optimization. One of the essential points regarding SEO is the number of key words utilized per page of content. Changing/updating the content on your website plays an important role in getting you noticed. There is work involved in doing this and frankly, there is no truly easy way out.

Deciding you want to go down this road requires a professional who understands the mechanisms of this process. You want to find someone with a proven track record in tailoring the information you have to present, in a way that makes sense and raises your website's profile in web searches related to your business. I have utilized a couple of different services over the years and will do so again in the future; as I fine tune the various websites I maintain to attract new business. I find it a worthwhile expense, as it is not something I desire to become proficient at myself.

REASON #4: DATA DICTATE SUCCESS.

I'M A GEEK FOR DATA. Metrics, numbers, statistics have become intrinsically significant in being sign posts in two areas of my business. I know who to contact, for what reasons, and generally what trends to expect during each season of the year. I can hear your brain rattling at this point with the following question. How does this get my business more customers? Ah, I'm so glad you asked.

First off this doesn't happen overnight. Gathering data will take time. By tracking my guests' spending habits during the last few years, I've been able to identify which of my guests are interested in the variety of events I hold throughout the year. Data gathering in this case is a form of customer profiling. I collect essential identifying characteristics (gender, birthdates, job, etc....). These simple data points, along with other data I collect on my business afford me the opportunity to direct market to wider audiences by targeting groups with similar characteristics.

By leveraging this data for instance, I can boost a post on Facebook targeting several groups with similar sets of characteristics.

Perhaps this is a bit oversimplified, but it hits the highlights of what I'm doing. I can tell you, it has garnered me new guests for much less investment than it would have taken otherwise. In the restaurant world, it's much easier to keep guests than it is to find new ones, and it costs much less money as well. By knowing the metrics surrounding my current guests, I have more power to search for new ones at much less expense.

Certainly if you're just starting out with no customer base to begin with you won't be able to do this level of target marketing. However, if you're wise, your particular industry may have general data you can utilize to your advantage to gain your first clients/customers before you even open your doors.

Reason #5: You're not the nosey neighbor.

A GOOD NUMBER OF married couples struggle with one or the other's parents constantly butting into their private life. While well-meaning or as good intentioned your in-laws may be, having a buttinsky in your life is no fun, adds stress, and in the end is not generally a truly value added force.

An important key to understanding, the dichotomy between being a Nosey Norman/Nancy, and the notion of value added, is knowing what value you're looking for. You want to be a Nosey Norman/Nancy, and you don't have to necessarily hide your motives, be obnoxious, or become James Bond. Whether you're out and about with your family, on vacation, attending trade/industry shows, or in your local competition's company; being aware and gathering information is crucial to being the nosey neighbor that adds value to your own business.

Your goal is to gather as much information as you can about your competition so you stay informed and up-to-date regarding what is going on in your industry/business at local, regional, and national levels. Hopefully it is obvious that knowing what your closest local competitor(s) is/are doing, will position you to target market more effectively, and/or create a service or services that did not previously exist: giving you the edge. Among your goals should also be a focus on how you can find a niche that affords you the opportunity to edge out your competition. You may offer an identical type of service, and figuring out how you can add value for your customers that your competition is not offering, will invariably make your business/service/product more desirable to seek out.

REASON #6: WHAT LIGHT'S YOUR FIRE? WHERE'S YOUR PASSION?

PASSION, OR THE LACK thereof drives me crazy. I see way too many business owners not displaying any true passion for their businesses. In part there is some direct correlation for the employees of these businesses not having passion as well. A great deal can be said for the "Wow" factor, when you walk into an establishment where the employees and the owner(s) are engaged, happy to be there, knowledgeable, and passionate about what they represent. The same enthusiasm, though a bit trickier to pull off, can and should be demonstrated or represented through your website as well.

When I walk into a business I'm looking to be wowed in some manner. Your product/service, regardless of what it may be, is just as important as the atmosphere/ethos you present it in. Remember, it costs you more to get customers in your establishment the first time. Once there, you want them to become repeat, regular customers and Pied Pipers of referrals for new business. (Hopefully, you already know referrals are the least expensive means of gaining new business.)

According to Merriam-Webster.com, passion is a strong feeling of enthusiasm or excitement for something or doing something. I want you to not only be aware of this definition, but I want you to live it regarding your business and have it spill over into other areas of your life. Passion for life is contagious and more often than not, very successful people tend to also be highly passionate individuals.

With concerns over unsafe manufacturing practices in foreign companies, many US citizens have gravitated in recent years to US made and produced products whenever possible. Embedded in the concern regarding unsafe/unhealthy products from abroad, is the desire to seek out and support more locally produced high quality products within our economy. I'm not here to present political ideologies, but rather make a point regarding how ideas can be used as a passionate and targeted marketing plan with great effect.

I hardly ever use medications, preferring a natural approach to everything in my life. There may be times when it becomes necessary to deviate from that path. I had such a need a couple of years back for a pharmacy based product. Since I'm not familiar with our local pharmacies, I began to inquire. I consistently heard from several individuals with whom I made inquiries, that one of the local pharmacies was more expensive than the others and to stay clear of them. This honestly had the opposite effect. I went to that pharmacy, spoke with the pharmacist and practically had to grill him to get to the bottom of why he was more expensive than anyone else around for the "same" prescriptions.

After interviewing him for some time, I finally learned he would source ONLY American made and produced pharmaceuticals. He had done a good deal of research, kept up with latest developments in his industry, and where the items he needed were made. He was not simply convinced, but passionately convinced it was in the best interest and safety of his clientele to only purvey materials from US based labs. His overall demeanor was not outwardly passionate, until he began sharing the information he learned.

Would you agree with me, this man has a deep passion and concern for his clientele? Would you agree his concern and passion for his clientele could turn into a major source of marketing and over time only serve his business in the best possible way? Sadly, no one really knew the full story for his higher pricing and this was hurting him to a greater extent than the other way around.

Simple signage throughout his pharmacy highlighting his underlying passion, "Drugs made and produced in the USA ONLY", would nearly instantly gain him new business and nearly instantly dispel the common public view, that he was only just a higher priced pharmacy for nothing more or less than the value of what you'd get elsewhere. If this pharmacist added simple signage on ALL the products on the shelves in his establishment that were US made and produced; he'd quickly find himself and his business in a completely new place in the community's view and find himself in better financial position.

The foregoing simple adjustments go to marketing, expressing his story, and targeting a specific market/customer profile. By making these simple adjustments this pharmacist could unleash his passion as a true win-win for his customers and his business. Ultimately he would gain many new customers, who would more than happily spend the extra 10%, knowing what they're using is safer, cleaner, and made in the USA. This pharmacist won my business over the others in the area, though he'd never get rich from my family or me. After learning about this man's passion and ethic, I've gone one step further on his behalf. I've become a Pied Piper for his business when anyone else may inquire with me regarding the need for a pharmacist's services.

Reason #7: What's your story?

STORYTELLING AND passion are stable mates though the two should not be confused. People love to be "in the know" and through the use of storytelling you can make the whys and hows of your business significantly more memorable, unique, and accessible to your clientele.

Storytelling is a powerful form of marketing. People want to know the whys and hows of your business. Actually, it can go far beyond your business. In my case people like to know my first memories of cooking with my grandmother when I was four years old. They also like to know the details of my journey through alternative health and how it transformed my career to build a business offering superbly cooked real food; and presenting unique family owned/operated companies producing the wide variety of small batch beverages on our menu. My guests have come to anticipate and even expect new stories related to our visits to vineyards, breweries, distilleries, farms, and manufacturers. They're not surprised at all when I share something regarding a product or service completely unrelated to the restaurant, but is part of something I'm passionate about outside of my business. I love sharing the story behind "X" product or service.

Let me state emphatically storytelling is NOT lying or embellishing the truth. I'm advocating for truthful, accurate storytelling that conveys passionately the necessary information regarding the service(s) or product presented.

I fully believe everyone has a story to tell regarding the reason for being in business and the product(s) they represent or the service(s) they offer. The truth is: there is only one of you. You are unique. You have your own flair. You have your own voice. You have your own approach which sets you apart. You have expertise. You are the only you: doing what you do.

The sad thing is, people don't think of themselves as unique and this speaks to a lack of confidence. Your story is important and potentially critical to the success of your business. Remember, what may be "normal" to you is NOT necessarily normal to anyone else, and potentially of significant interest. I frequently ask business owners I meet the question: "What got you interested in doing this?"

So, how do you tell your story? In the world of modern technology and social media, getting your story our there is significantly easier than it has ever been. Sharing your story can be done anyplace and at any time. The best place to share the story of your services, business, or product is of course face-to-face every time the opportunity to do so arises. Telling your story to potentially new clients/customers or a returning one who has not seen you in sometime, or hasn't heard it before makes for the ideal. I emphasize face-to-face sharing is the best possible way to share your story because it is a great tool for making or closing a sale.

I frequent a local runner's supply shop. I'm passionate about outdoor fitness activities, a good many of the guests in my restaurant know this and many share in my passion. The place I seek out most of my related equipment is owned and operated by Frank Giannino. When you walk into Frank's shop, there is a large map of the United States on the wall that no one could possibly miss. Clearly marked on the map are two routes from San Francisco to New York. Both of these routes signify Frank's trans-America running journeys. Both Frank's passion and his story took serious form in 1979 when he ran across America twice. In fact, Frank set a record in 1980 that stood until 2016. Think about how profound the length of Frank's record was: 36 years! What a story he has to share.

Frank published a book entitled, **46 Days**, displayed on his counter, also for all to see. Aside from Frank's story being communicated non-verbally through these displays, he's happy to share aspects of his journey to any who inquire. Additionally, it is clear from the manner in which he treats and attends to each of his customers when asking questions about their intended training goals, running style, and foot fit needs/desires: Frank is a man of passion, knowledge and care. All of these reasons come together in a complete package that keep him sought after and busy, and keep me recommending first and foremost to anyone who wants to get into running.

Of course we are in the digital age, and social media reach through the thoughtful use of the Internet is a seriously powerful tool to tell a story. Honestly, the possibilities here are nearly endless. The first and most obvious place to get your story into the marketplace is through your website. The "About" page should have your story in an engaging and concise manner. Lengthier expression of your story can be moved to another page or section of your website: make sure it is clear there is more to learn. Be creative in this effort, but also be thoroughly honest. Depending upon the type of business you're running, you might have a blog. A blog won't only just reach the interested clientele you have; it will eventually garner search results helping you obtain new customers.

Linking your website, blog, story page, about information, etc....to your Facebook, Twitter, YouTube, and LinkedIn accounts will also help generate interest in your business, services, and/or product(s). I'm a huge fan of sharing information via video, so I have a rather large YouTube account linked to all of the other social media outlets I utilize.

If you're still finding you're stuck and don't truly feel you have a real story to tell then perhaps you might pick up a copy of Seth Godin's book, *All Marketers ~~Are Liars~~ Tell Stories: The Underground Classic that Explains How Marketing Really Works – and Why Authenticity Is the Best Marketing of All.* By understanding the key elements of how to properly develop a means of sharing your passion through an honest story, leveraging all the elements of a good story; you'll be able to more effectively reach a broader market and earn new customers.

Reason #8: Market your business like you'd spread grass seed: Network

GETTING PEOPLE TO SEE and hear about your business is of course how you're going to get new customers. There are traditional methods of advertising, many of which are rather costly. We all know the best means of obtaining new customers is through referrals and word of mouth. You need to be one of the loudest promoters of your business: doing so with confidence. The technique known as networking is one of those methods of accomplishing this for your business.

When I first opened my restaurant fourteen years ago (at the time of this writing), I belonged to quite a few networking groups. Some of you may not be familiar with these groups. Local Chambers of Commerce and local business development groups would advertise and set these up. Generally these were pre-workday groups meeting for breakfast, though meeting times could vary, and were held once or twice a month. The purpose of these groups was to meet others not in your field/industry, make contacts and in the process expand your sphere of influence and recognition. I was a member of quite a few different groups.

At first I went to almost every one of these gathering I was invited to. It was about spending face-to-face time with as many people as possible. Some of these were in my area and some of them were 30 to 45 minutes away. At the time, distance wasn't necessarily a factor, as it was more important for me to be in front of as diverse an audience as I could. As a restaurateur, I was invited to participate in a variety of tasting events where we could present our cuisine. I jumped at almost all of these opportunities as well. Fourteen years later, I still network, but not necessarily in the same ways or with the same sense of urgency as I once had.

First of all, I'm seriously proud of my success in the restaurant business and take great pride in products my restaurant represents. From the time a guest (new or regular) walks in to the time they leave I know they will have a superior dining experience, because of the confidence I have in my staff's working knowledge of nearly everything that goes on in the restaurant from front of house to the kitchen. Our guests are greeted as if they're family walking through the front door of our home. The reason I share the foregoing is because I am simply that proud of what my wife and I have established. So, when I speak to people at conferences, trade shows, tastings, events, or wherever I may be in the moment; if I can comfortably work my business into the conversation I will.

The awareness and ability to self-promote is in fact a form of networking. In my opinion, the ability to plant the seeds (your enthusiasm and passion) and have your business card always handy (visual reminder for later reference) will lead to gaining new customers/clientele. Once that new customer is through your door (brick and mortar or virtual) you must deliver the goods that brought them to you in the first place: your superior expertise, enthusiasm, passion, and integrity.

Of course, when you're starting out as a newbie business owner, you still may want to attend the aforementioned Chamber of Commerce and/or local business development group meetings. But, I believe once you've done a couple of these, you owe it to yourself to forge more creative paths in this area of networking. These paths will include the times you're purchasing the services of someone else's business, be it when purchasing a new car, fire wood, having the plumber stop in, being at the doctor's office, etc... All interactions are potentials for widening your sphere of influence with someone who knows people you don't and might require the services or products you're offering.

Further opportunities for networking your business include the charitable activities in which you engage. I believe in the notion of paying it forward and have been directly involved in some charitable activity since the very first year we opened our business. In fact, the first meal we served in my restaurant was to support those less fortunate. We hosted a soup kitchen prior to our official commercial grand opening. We have been serving our community in this manner every Christmas season since our first year. The number of families in need to whom we've delivered complete dinners has steadily increased over the years. We partner with a local social service agency to more efficiently coordinate these efforts. We enlist the help of our guests as volunteers to help cook, package, and deliver these meals. This has been a tremendous boon to my restaurant from a variety of perspectives, and it never ceases to amaze me year after year we meet new people who become regular guests as a result of this effort. It is an outstandingly positive win-win scenario.

Your business may not be able to cater directly to families in need, but you may find yourself volunteering for an organization you're passionate about. You can make this a core charity benefitting from your labor (some donation from your business) and from your hands on involvement when the need of that organization requires it. You're creating a win-win by networking in this area and further embedding the value of your presence in the community at large.

Reason #9: How mobile is your presence?

YOU HAVE A WEBSITE and that is an essential tool in today's market place. You keep it up-to-date and you've invested in optimizing your presence on the worldwide web with help in the area of SEO. Cool. But more and more people are on significantly smaller devices than their laptop and/or desktop computers. So, what do you do?

As with exploring SEO, you're going to have to explore optimizing your website to be easily viewed on the small screens of handheld devices. The background coding for this to be accomplished is a bit different than it is when you're programming a website for viewing on larger platforms with more memory and expanded software coding.

Again, I'm not an expert in this field, but I am painfully aware of how my old, out dated original restaurant website was not mobile friendly. While I am keen to utilize technology to its fullest, I waited way too long to change our restaurant's website. I began making a transition two years ago with the assistance of a couple of people who are experts in this area. In the interim I had consulted for and helped launch another restaurant. During the new restaurant's construction phase, we did our due diligence and also constructed its website for both large and small format viewing from the outset.

As someone who enjoys being very hands on, I immersed myself in the process, keeping up with the consultants we engaged. By the time we opened the doors to the new restaurant I had learned a great deal. I became savvier regarding what makes websites more efficient and mobile friendly. The result was a complete rebuild and presentation style for the wealth of content I had posted to our restaurant's website over the fourteen years we've been in business.

You need to know. If you're doing this from scratch, that is, just starting out developing your business' website and developing the content for it, you're in a much stronger position. Stay there, by staying organized at the outset. Having to reorganize with a wealth of content later on can be an enormous time eater.

Again, as with SEO fine tuning of your business' web presence, you'll want to get someone else's help in either constructing or reconstructing your website. If you're up for the challenge and the related frustrations that will invariably go along the experience, then dive right in yourself to make your website more mobile friendly. The effort or expense (time vs money as the case may be), will be more than worth it. Both your current clientele and the ones who've yet find you for the first time; will be readily able to read, view, and contact you with a properly done mobile presence.

Reason #10: Who's Your Audience?

YOUR BUSINESS IS OPEN, you've given long hard thought to what it looks like and what service or products you're going to offer. But have you considered who your audience is?

I opened a restaurant. I have a deep love for cooking and have had one since I was a youngster learning from my grandmother. I've worked every job within the restaurant industry over the years. Frankly, I couldn't think of anything else I'd rather do. I spend just about every day in my restaurant and am very proud of what I've created. My staff is well trained and to be honest, I don't need to be there every day. I've developed every aspect of my establishment to be able to run without me for two, possibly more weeks at a time if I so choose or needed to take the time off.

I don't share the foregoing to gloat: the exact opposite. I share the foregoing because I want to illustrate a couple of points based on knowing your audience. You need to know to whom you're marketing your business. The more clear you are about who your primary clientele is either now or in the near future, will help inform/direct/guide the manner in which you gain new business, earn a positive reputation, build upon your success, and know how to handle all the inevitable issues that will arise. Also, it will help guide you in your hiring processes, develop your policies and procedures, and a host of other aspects of your business you may not have given much thought to at this point.

Don't think of this as the tail wagging the dog, as the expression goes. You are in business to make money. You are in business to be successful. Hopefully, you're in business to be able to provide opportunity for others, which can be found in the replication of your efforts by hiring others to be able to do what you do well.

In my restaurant I cater to those who care about the food they eat, are generally not in a rush, want to know where their food comes from, will pay for quality, want an outstanding dining experience, and don't want the pretense of having to wear a suit or gown. My guests essentially come to my house, sit at my dining table, and eat the healthy food I happily and confidently serve to my family. I can readily stand behind every item offered in my restaurant. Let me say that again. I can stand behind every item I offer. How many business owners can do that?

I knew there was an audience out there to support my beliefs and there were enough of them to make my business a lucrative effort. Getting to this place didn't happen overnight. It took time, research, and I had to grow in my own confidence to be able to carry this out. Once I hit my stride, the people I hired and the procedures I instituted definitely had to change to support my efforts.

So, I'll ask you again: Who is your audience? How will you reach them? How will you stay the course and develop your audience so in the end, you have a means of converting others to your methodology, services rendered, products offered?

Reason #11: Don't Put All Your Money in One Place.

When I promote my business, especially from the perspective of "advertising" I don't put all my efforts in one place only. In her article, Hannah Whittenly, noted,

"When a particular marketing technique pays off, it's tempting to go all-in and to focus all of your budget and efforts on it. However, this can and will backfire in a number of ways. Diversification is crucial when it comes to effectively marketing a business."

I emphatically concur with her. When I first opened my restaurant I used "traditional" advertising routes that didn't yield particularly good results. The one or two that did were tempting to focus on. Thankfully, I knew a bit better even then. I encourage you to pay heed to this advice.

Your mother or father or one of your grandparents probably told you to, "never put all your eggs in one basket." It's an often stated bit of wisdom that applies to many areas of our lives. For those of you who are not familiar with this aphorism, it simply means you shouldn't rely on one particular thing for results every time. Literally speaking, putting all of your eggs in one basket could result in losing all of those eggs if you drop the basket.

Life is about diversity of effort. You certainly don't want to scatter your efforts so widely that you're spread thin to the point of breaking and not yielding any results. But as with anything else, you want to target your efforts to maximize your resources: read that as dollars spent to earn more coin. This can come from trial and error with regard to advertising your business or you can be a bit more surgical about it.

Recall, I think of myself as a bit of data geek. I like a surgical approach based upon data from past results. In my business we target market our audience through a variety of means. As previously mentioned, I gather data regularly. By knowing who attends our events, how often they dine in our restaurant, how they respond to their experience(s) with us through surveys, etc.; I know how to target my audience and actually save money while making money at the same time.

Venues like Instagram, Facebook, and Twitter can serve as excellent advertising venues for very little investment. While you may start out purchasing an advert or two in your local paper or purchase a short radio spot or two on your local radio station to get you "out there" in the public conscience; you'll find very quickly your return on investment (ROI) is not going to be as high as the social media venues. Couple this with knowing your audience and getting those referrals I've mentioned previously and you have a very solid foundation on which to build a financial future with your business.

Exercise your creativity when targeting diverse advertising outlets so you capture the essence of who you are and what you represent to grab your audience's attention.

Reason #12: What makes you unique?

This section is a bit of an agglomeration of a couple of the previous ones and it's worth having it standing alone. You've successfully discovered your story and your passion. Certainly these two things make you unique. I think there's a bit of a deeper well to dig in order to make you the standout in your field.

Being a generalist is not by any stretch of the imagination a bad thing. In fact, it can be the opposite. However, in today's market place being a good generalist may hurt your business because there are other good generalists in your locale as well. Within your field what makes you a standout is you're the expert for one or two problems that may typically arise. During a recent trip to Florida I heard the owner of an air conditioning service company on the radio explaining how the competition, generally speaking, did not know how to properly tune up a home's central air conditioning system. Not knowing any better, this sounded to me like it would be the job of a good a/c generalist.

The owner of the company spoke at length on the points related to and the reasons why his services were unique, why his company was superior, and the lengths beyond his competition his employees go to ensure their service was superior. I know nothing about home air conditioning systems. I know that living in Florida, any home without a properly working system will suffer mold issues, the occupants will suffer potential health issues, and there can be potential property loss because of the humidity in the home.

After listening to this business owner speak for about twenty minutes he had me sold. Frankly, if I lived in this area of Florida, I'd definitely have called the company to have one of their service agents evaluate my home's a/c system. It made even more sense to me; to ensure that one of the most significant investments someone makes, their home, is properly maintained to the highest level, not just for the sake of the investment, but more importantly for the health and safety of one's family.

Certainly you had to be there listening to appreciate what I heard. But I can share with you; this man spoke with authority, assurance, confidence, and what clearly came across as experience in his field of expertise. There was no trace of arrogance: just the solid confidence of someone with deep knowledge.

In this example, he was using his ability to diagnose a home air conditioning system to its finest level of detail when conducting this "proprietary" tune up. He trained his staff on site to his level of expertise (replication of himself) and sought to hire people who already had a deep understanding of understood customer service. In fact, and this is part of what really grabbed my attention: he stated that he sought to hire people from the restaurant service industry with very high end experience because they didn't have to be taught customer service.

Do you get what he said? He emphatically stated he could train anyone to service an air conditioning system. He also emphatically stated he could not truly teach or impart the value of customer service to someone who did not already gravitate towards those ideals.

So what makes this business owner unique is multifold. He knows this. He clearly articulated these characteristics and has built a series of systems through which to demonstrate and deliver the goods to his customer base. You understand that I found this individual rather impressive in his confidence and apparent knowledge base. It was clear to me he knows exactly what he's doing in order to present himself as unique in an area that has both saturation of other related businesses and need for said business.

It is your job, if not your mission, to develop your own skills, services, and product offerings to be able to set you apart in the market you're catering to. When you can do this well, you'll not only stand out as the expert to do business with, you'll potentially have other businesses coming to you to teach them to do likewise.

Final Thoughts

The foregoing are but a dozen of a host of ways you can help your business gain new customers, while also help secure the ones you currently have. Truly you are the captain of your own ship and how you navigate the waters of the industry you're operating in is completely up to you. Staying alert to the obstacles before you, the shortfalls of your personality and knowledge base, and using almost everything and anything at your disposal as an opportunity, will be critical for your overall success.

I know the foregoing sounds like just another coach spewing meaningless platitudes. Frankly, that couldn't be further from the truth. I truly live and eat what I've presented to you. I've shared how I've revamped our website and hired a consultant to further refine our SEO efforts so my various websites would see greater traffic and thereby position me to be able to obtain new customers. Those of you who follow me on

Facebook or YouTube will know that I regularly put up new content because I have seen how relevant and/or related content can drive traffic back to my websites, and build upon the successes I already have.

I stay current by either reading or listening to a variety of books in the areas of motivation and business success. I learn a good deal of where to find this information by having subscribed to services like Google Alerts. Knowledge for me is truly important, especially in the areas where I'm seeking success and am currently not as strong or knowledgeable as I want to be. I'm doing this all while staying alert and seeking to better understand the audience I'm presenting to; using true stories from my own experiences to hopefully capture the imaginations/interests of others, while at the same time be motivating to them.

Let me close this by saying: I'm no saint and I'm not perfect by a long shot. I'm just a guy, a husband, a father, a business owner who truly wants more for his family, himself, and his employees. I'm hugely into just about all things related to a healthy lifestyle. This journey to success is very much like working out. It's tough to get started, but once you do, the whole experience becomes addicting. The key is just starting. I'm hoping that you'll find inspiration and motivation to get your business moving in the direction you want. By using the tools presented here, you could be well on your way to discovering there's a much deeper customer base for your business than you've ever imagined before.